Fact Finders®

EXPLORING HISTORY THROUGH FOOD

PIONEER FARM COOKING

by Mary Gunderson

CAPSTONE PRESS
a capstone imprint

Fact Finder Books are published by Capstone Press,
1710 Roe Crest Drive, North Mankato, Minnesota 56003.
www.mycapstone.com

Library of Congress Cataloging-in-Publication Data
Names: Gunderson, Mary, author.
Title: Pioneer farm cooking / by Mary Gunderson.
Description: North Mankato, Minnesota: Capstone Press, [2017] |
Series: Fact finders. Exploring history through food | Previous edition: Pioneer farm cooking / by Mary
   Gunderson (Mankato, MN : Blue Earth Books, c2000). | Includes bibliographical references and index.
Identifiers: LCCN 2015051231| ISBN 9781515723554 (library binding) |
   ISBN 9781515723592 (ebook pdf)
Subjects: LCSH: Cooking, American—Midwestern style--History—Juvenile literature. |
   Food habits—Middle West—History—19th century—Juvenile literature. |
   Frontier and pioneer life—Middle West—Juvenile literature. | LCGFT: Cookbooks.
Classification: LCC TX715.2.M53 G86 2017 | DDC 641.5977—dc23
LC record available at http://lccn.loc.gov/2015051231

Editorial Credits
Editor: Nikki Potts
Designer: Kayla Rossow
Media Researcher: Jo Miller
Production Specialist: Steve Walker

Photo Credits
Bridgeman Images: Private Collection/Peter Newark American Pictures, 9; Capstone Studio: Karon
Dubke, back cover (snow cone and chicken soup), 1 (snow cone and chicken soup), 20, 29; Getty
Images: Archive Photos/American Stock, 6, Photolibrary/Heather Weston, 1 (pickles), 15; Granger,
NYC - All rights reserved, 13; North Wind Picture Archives, cover (inset); Shutterstock: Agnes
Kantaruk, cover (cucumbers and background), Charles Knowles, 11, Dimedrol68, 14, Elena Veselova, 24,
Everett Historical, 8, 19, Foodstocker, back cover (potatoes), 27, rj lerich, 17, simonidad, 1 (pudding), 23

Design Elements
Shutterstock: 4Max, Amawasri Pakdara, Mliberra, Vitaly Korovin

Printed and bound in the USA
009670CGF16

TABLE OF CONTENTS

KITCHEN SAFETY

1. Make sure your hair and clothes will not be in the way while you are cooking.
2. Keep a fire extinguisher in the kitchen. Never put water on a grease fire.
3. Wash your hands with soap before you start to cook. Wash your hands with soap again after you handle meat or poultry.
4. Ask an adult for help with sharp knives, the stove, the oven, and all electrical appliances.
5. Turn handles of pots and pans to the middle of the stove. A person walking by could run into handles that stick out toward the room.
6. Use pot holders to take dishes out of the oven.
7. Wash all fruits and vegetables.
8. Always use a clean cutting board. Wash the cutting board thoroughly after cutting meat or poultry.
9. Wipe up spills immediately.
10. Store leftovers properly. Do not leave leftovers out at room temperature for more than two hours.

METRIC CONVERSION

U.S.	Canada	U.S.	Canada	Fahrenheit	Celsius
1 quart	1 liter	1/4 teaspoon	1 mL	325 degrees	160 degrees
1 ounce	30 grams	1/2 teaspoon	2 mL	350 degrees	180 degrees
2 ounces	55 grams	1 teaspoon	5 mL	375 degrees	190 degrees
4 ounces	85 gram	1 tablespoon	15 mL	400 degrees	200 degrees
1/2 pound	225 grams	1/4 cup	50 mL	425 degrees	220 degrees
1 pound	455 grams	1/3 cup	75 m		
		1/2 cup	125 mL		
		2/3 cup	150 mL		
		3/4 cup	175 mL		
		1 cup	250 mL		

COOKING EQUIPMENT

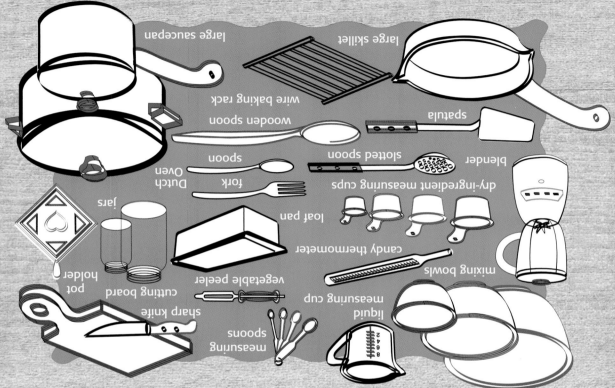

large saucepan

large skillet

wire baking rack

wooden spoon

spatula

spoon

slotted spoon

blender

Dutch Oven

fork

dry-ingredient measuring cups

jars

loaf pan

candy thermometer

mixing bowls

pot holder

cutting board

vegetable peeler

liquid measuring cup

sharp knife

measuring spoons

CHAPTER 1

A PIONEER HOME

Before the 1800s few U.S. citizens lived on the Great Plains. This area of the United States included parts of what are now the states of Montana, North Dakota, South Dakota, Wyoming, Nebraska, Kansas, Colorado, Oklahoma, New Mexico, and Texas. Most of this land was flat ground covered with prairie grass.

The U.S. government wanted people to settle the Great Plains. To encourage farmers to move to this unsettled **territory**, the U.S. government passed the Homestead Act of 1862. Through this law the government promised 160 acres (65 hectares) of free land to anyone who lived on and worked the land for five years.

Farmers traveled across the open plains in wagon trains to claim land on the Great Plains.

territory—any large area of land; a region

Settling the Great Plains was hard work. Pioneers traveled by covered wagon for several months across hundreds of miles to reach their land. Few towns existed on the Great Plains in the 1860s. After arriving, pioneers had to build shelters and homes. They used materials found in the surrounding forests or prairies.

THE GREAT PLAINS REGION MAP

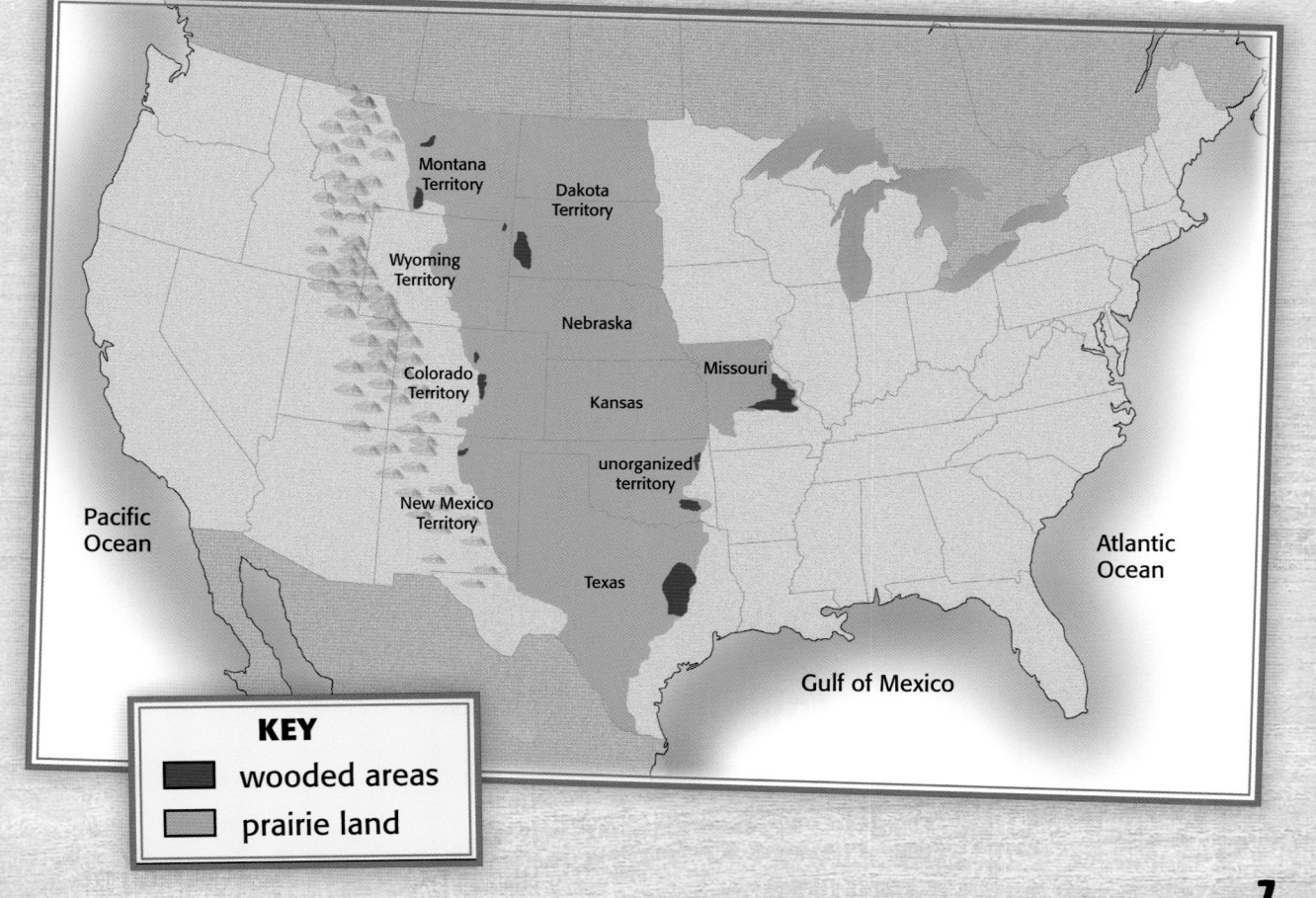

Montana Territory

Dakota Territory

Wyoming Territory

Nebraska

Colorado Territory

Missouri

Kansas

unorganized territory

New Mexico Territory

Pacific Ocean

Texas

Atlantic Ocean

Gulf of Mexico

KEY
- wooded areas
- prairie land

Pioneers who settled in wooded areas cut down trees to build log homes. The most common log home was a square or rectangular cabin with one room. Early settlers built a stone or clay fireplace at one end of the cabin for cooking and heating.

A family of homesteaders poses in front of their sod home in Nebraska.

In the prairie regions of the Great Plains, trees were scarce. Pioneers used blocks of earth and grass called sod to build their homes. They used a special plow to cut strips of sod. Then they cut the strips into sod blocks. Sod bricks were then stacked to make walls. Pioneers called their sod homes "**soddys**."

Thick, sturdy sod was not always available in large quantities. Many pioneers dug out the side of a hill and sealed the front with sod blocks. The dugouts gave families protection from the wind and the cold. Inside, pioneers stomped down the soil to make a hard floor. Some women made rag rugs to lay over the floor.

soddy—pioneer homes made from stacking strips and blocks of sod

CHAPTER 2

THE COOKSTOVE

Many pioneers used cookstoves for cooking food and heating their homes in the late 1800s. Women did much of the cooking on the farm. They used cookstoves for many purposes. While roasts cooked in the oven, vegetables boiled on stovetop plates. Warming ovens extended over the stovetop to keep pies and breads warm until dinnertime. Some cookstoves had **water reservoirs** attached to their side. These hot water tanks kept the water warm throughout the day.

Cookstoves were kept burning most of the time. Where wood was plentiful, it was used for fuel. For fast cooking, pioneers burned dry oak or another dry wood. They used green wood, or wood that had not completely dried, for slow cooking.

A pioneer woman cooks dinner.

HOMEMADE BREAD

INGREDIENTS

2-1/2 cups warm water
   at 120°F (49°C)
2 tablespoons butter
4 cups all-purpose flour,
   divided in half
1-1/2 teaspoons salt
1 teaspoon sugar
1 package active dry yeast
   (2-1/4 teaspoons)
1-1/2 cups whole wheat flour
1/2 to 3/4 cup all-purpose flour
   for kneading
3 tablespoons butter or margarine

EQUIPMENT

2 large mixing bowls
wooden spoon
candy thermometer
liquid measuring cup
dry-ingredient measuring cups
measuring spoons
clean dish towel
cutting board
3 paper towels or napkins
2 loaf pans, 9-inches by 5-inches
   (23-centimeters by 13-cm)
pot holders
wire baking rack

Ask an adult to help you make this recipe.

1. In bowl, combine 2-1/2 cups water at 120°F (49°C) (use thermometer with an
   adult's help to test the water), 2 tablespoons butter, 2 cups all-purpose flour,
   1-1/2 teaspoons salt, and 1 teaspoon sugar. Stir to mix.

2. Add package of yeast. Beat 3 minutes or until smooth.

3. Cover with towel. Let stand at room temperature for 30 minutes.

4. Gradually stir in remaining 2 cups all-purpose flour and 1-1/2 cups whole
   wheat flour. Turn dough out of bowl onto lightly floured cutting board
   or clean countertop.

5. Sprinkle flour on dough. Knead dough 7 to 10 minutes.
   Add flour if dough sticks to your hands.

6. Use one paper towel or napkin dabbed with 1 tablespoon butter or margarine to lightly grease second bowl.

7. Place dough in bowl. Roll dough around to moisten surface. Cover with towel. Set in warm place to rise. Let dough rise 50 to 60 minutes or until doubled in size. Check dough by gently pressing your fingertip into the dough. If the shape of your fingertip remains, the dough is ready.

8. Press dough to flatten out air bubbles. Lightly knead dough a few times in bowl. Divide dough in half and shape each half into a ball.

9. Grease two loaf pans using 1 tablespoon butter or margarine for each. Press each ball of dough flat, then roll tightly to make a tube about as long as the bread pan. Tuck ends under. Place dough in pan with smooth side up.

10. Cover loaves with towel. Let dough rise about 45 minutes or until doubled in size. Press one of the loaves gently with a fingertip. When shape of fingertip remains, loaves are ready to bake.

11. Heat oven to 375°F (190°C). Bake loaves 45 minutes or until golden brown. Remove bread from pans. Cool on wire baking rack. (Ask an adult to place and remove the bread from the oven and help you take it out of the pans.)

Makes 2 loaves.

CHAPTER 3

FROM GARDEN TO TABLE

Pioneers planted large vegetable gardens near their farmhouses. They saved the seeds from plants and used them year after year. Some foods, such as onions, horseradish, and various spices, seeded themselves and sprouted each year without replanting. Vegetable gardens provided fresh vegetables and herbs. Pioneers planted beans, carrots, peas, lettuce, cabbages, and cucumbers. They also grew squash, potatoes, sweet potatoes, and tomatoes. They dried and canned the foods to eat during the winter.

CORN, THE ALL-AROUND VEGETABLE

Corn was the main vegetable eaten by pioneers. It was easy to grow and pick. Pioneers cooked corn in a variety of ways. If the corn was fresh, pioneers removed the husks and silk and boiled the ears in a pot. Others preferred to boil or roast the corn with the ears still in the husks. Corn kernels were also cut from the cob with a sharp knife, mixed with milk or butter, and fried in pork or bacon fat.

Pioneers canned and dried vegetables as they ripened during the summer. Many of the vegetables needed to be saved for the fall and winter months when fresh food was not available. Pioneers shelled and dried beans and peas and poured them

Homesteaders plow the corn field in front of their home in Custer County, Nebraska.

into sacks. Kernels of corn were set in the sun to dry. Pioneers hung strings of onion to dry and packed all the vegetables in a **root cellar** for later use.

Women preserved some vegetables in glass jars. This process was called canning. Women canned tomatoes, sweet corn, and beets. They boiled the fresh vegetables with salt and pepper or fried them in **lard**. Then they dumped the vegetables into hot jars and sealed the jars with lids.

Pioneers also canned sauerkraut and pickles. Women pickled cucumbers in jars of vinegar, salt, and dill. To give the pickles a sweet taste, pioneers sometimes added sugar and spices.

root cellar—a hole dug out of the ground or into the side of a hill. Used to store jars of canned food and bundles of dried herbs and plants
lard—a solid white grease made from the melted-down fat of pigs and hogs. Lard is used in cooking

BREAD AND BUTTER PICKLES

INGREDIENTS

5 to 6 cucumbers
2 large white onions
1-1/2 cups white vinegar
2 cups granulated sugar
2 tablespoons canning salt
1 teaspoon of turmeric
1 teaspoon mustard seed
1/2 teaspoon celery seed

EQUIPMENT

sharp knife
cutting board
large bowl with lid or plastic wrap
medium bowl
liquid measuring cup
dry-ingredient measuring cups
measuring spoons
wooden spoon
small jars with tight-fitting lids
spoon

Ask an adult to help you make this recipe.

Day one:

1. Cut off ends of cucumbers. Slice cucumbers about 1/4-inch (0.6-cm) thick. (Ask an adult to help you with this step.)

2. Peel skin from onions. Slice onions very thin. Place a layer of cucumbers on the bottom of a large bowl. Cover the cucumbers with onions. Repeat layers until all cucumbers and onions are used.

3. In medium bowl, combine 1-1/2 cups vinegar, 2 cups sugar, 2 tablespoons canning salt, 1 teaspoon turmeric, 1 teaspoon mustard seed, and 1/2 teaspoon celery seed. Stir gently until sugar and salt dissolve in vinegar. Pour over cucumbers and onions.

4. Cover the bowl with lid or plastic wrap and place in refrigerator overnight.

Day two:

1. Dish up and eat.

2. Spoon leftover pickles with liquid into jars. Cover with tight-fitting lids. Store in refrigerator up to one month.

Makes about 8 cups of pickles.

CHAPTER 4

LIVESTOCK ON THE FARM

Pioneers depended on livestock as a source of food and clothing. Many brought hogs, chickens, cows, and sometimes sheep or goats to their new homes.

Cows supplied pioneers with milk. They drank the milk and used **buttermilk** to make biscuits, breads, and sweets. Butter made from milk was placed on the table for every meal. After the cows were too old to produce milk, they were butchered for meat and clothing. The meat was cut into steaks and roasts. Pioneers tanned hide into leather for shoes.

Chickens provided the family with eggs. Pioneers who lived near towns traded chicken eggs for flour, sugar, or coffee beans at the **general store**.

Some people built barns or shelters for their farm animals. Some let their animals roam freely on the land until they could find enough wood to build a fence. Children herded the animals and brought them home at the end of each day.

buttermilk—the sour liquid left over after butter has been churned from cream
general store—a store found in a small town, which sells many different things, including groceries

PORK SAUSAGE PATTIES

INGREDIENTS

1 pound lean
  ground pork
1/2 teaspoon salt
1/2 teaspoon ground
  black pepper

1 teaspoon dried,
  rubbed sage
1 teaspoon dried,
  crushed savory
1 teaspoon fennel seed

EQUIPMENT

large bowl
measuring spoons
wooden spoon
large skillet
spatula

Ask an adult to help you make this recipe.

1. In large bowl, combine 1 pound lean
   ground pork, 1/2 teaspoon salt,
   1/2 teaspoon black pepper,
   1 teaspoon sage, and
   1 teaspoon savory.

2. Add 1 teaspoon fennel seed
   by rubbing it between your
   hands over the bowl. Stir all
   ingredients to mix.

3. Divide mixture into 6 to 8 patties,
   about 4 inches (10 cm) across.

4. In large skillet over medium heat,
   cook sausage patties 3 to 4 minutes on each side until crisp and brown.
   (Ask an adult to help you with this step.)

Makes 6 to 8 servings.

CHAPTER 5

FAMILY CHORES

Pioneers grew much of the food they ate and made many household items, such as soap and furniture, from scratch.

Most men worked in the field, took care of the animals, and built the house and barns. They planted, weeded, and picked crops of corn and wheat. **Harvest** time was hard work for pioneer men. They did not have machines to cut and separate the crops. Much of this work was done with plows pulled by horses or oxen.

Women mainly did household and yard chores. They baked, canned, and dried food. They gathered eggs, picked fruits and vegetables, and watered the garden. They washed clothes by hand in a tub of hot water or in a nearby stream.

Older children watched the younger children while their mother worked. Children helped weed the garden, water and feed the animals, and churn butter. Women taught their daughters how to make meals and how to sew. Older boys followed their fathers to the fields to learn how to tend the crops.

harvest—to collect or gather up crops

CHURNING BUTTER

Pioneers made butter from cream. Most made their butter in a wooden churn. The churns were about 3 feet (91 cm) tall and about 1 foot (30 cm) wide. A butter churn had a stick called a dasher that stuck out of the lid. A dasher had two small wooden planks attached to one end in the shape of a cross. After cream had been poured into the churn, the lid was fitted on top of the churn.

Pioneers pulled, pushed, and rotated the dasher repeatedly until chunks of fat separated from the cream. Then the butter was removed from the churn and kneaded with a wooden paddle. They rinsed the butter with cold water until the water ran clear. If the buttermilk was not completely washed off, the butter soured within a few days.

a western Missouri pioneer homestead in 1820

CHICKEN SOUP WITH CORNMEAL DUMPLINGS

INGREDIENTS

Soup:
- 1 tablespoon vegetable oil
- 1 pound boneless,
    skinless chicken breasts
- 8 cups water
- 4 carrots
- 2 medium parsnips
- 1 large onion
- 4 chicken bouillon cubes
- 1 tablespoon white or cider vinegar
- 1/2 teaspoon salt
- 1/2 teaspoon pepper

Dumplings:
- 3/4 cup all-purpose flour
- 1/3 cup yellow cornmeal
- 1 teaspoon baking powder
- 1/2 teaspoon salt
- 1 egg
- 1/4 cup water

EQUIPMENT

- measuring spoons
- Dutch oven or large saucepan with lid
- liquid measuring cup
- wooden spoon
- vegetable peeler
- cutting board
- sharp knife
- slotted spoon
- 2 small bowls
- dry-ingredient measuring cups
- fork
- spoon

Ask an adult to help you prepare this recipe.

1. In Dutch oven or large saucepan, heat 1 tablespoon oil over medium-high heat. Add chicken and cook until lightly browned, 3 to 4 minutes per side.
2. Remove pan from heat. Slowly stir in 8 cups water.
3. Clean and peel carrots and parsnips. Cut each carrot and parsnip in half. Add to water.
4. Peel skin from onion. Cut onion in half. Add 1/2 onion to water.
5. Drop 4 bouillon cubes into water. Bring mixture to a boil.
6. Reduce heat to medium-low. Cover. Cook 15 to 30 minutes. Remove vegetables with slotted spoon and throw away.
7. Remove chicken with slotted spoon. Let cool slightly. Cut chicken into bit-sized pieces.
8. Chop remaining carrots, parsnips, and onion. Add chicken, vegetables, 1 tablespoon vinegar, 1/2 teaspoon salt, and 1/2 teaspoon pepper to broth. Bring to boil over medium-high heat. Reduce heat to low. Cover and cook 15 to 30 minutes.

While soup is cooking, prepare dumplings:

1. In small bowl, combine 3/4 cup flour, 1/3 cup cornmeal, 1 teaspoon baking powder, and 1/2 teaspoon salt.
2. In another bowl, beat together 1 egg and 1/4 cup water with a fork.
3. Pour egg mixture into flour mixture. Stir 10 to 15 strokes, just until flour mixture is moistened.
4. Gently place a spoonful of dough on top of the boiling soup without letting it sink. Make 8 dumplings this way.
5. Cover pan tightly. Do not peek during cooking time. Steam and heat will escape and dumplings will become hard and tough.
6. Return pan to high heat and bring to boil.
7. Reduce heat to medium-low; cook about 10 minutes. Makes 8 servings.

CHAPTER 6

DESSERTS FROM THE PRAIRIE

Pioneer families often saved pies, cakes, and other desserts for Sunday meals or special occasions. In northern areas pioneers picked blackberries, bitter **chokecherries**, grapes, and even wild apples and cherries to make into pies and cobblers. Some scraped the sweet insides out of cactuses and fried them. Pioneers who did not have fruit sometimes baked vinegar pies. They mixed vinegar, water, sugar, butter, and flour and poured the mixture into a piecrust. The finished pie had a jellylike filling and a tangy taste.

In pioneer times sugar was expensive, and sometimes the nearest store was many miles away. Most women bought brown sugar instead of white sugar because it was cheaper. Some grew **sorghum**. They cut down sorghum canes and extracted the juice inside. They then melted the juice down into a sugary syrup. Pioneers poured this sweet syrup on bread or added it to coffee.

chokecherry—a wild cherry with a bitter fruit that is nearly black when ripe
sorghum—a tropical grass that is cultivated for grain, forage, or syrup

RICE PUDDING WITH CINNAMON SUGAR

INGREDIENTS

Rice Pudding:

- 1 cup long-grain rice
- 1/4 teaspoon salt
- 2 cups water
- 4 cups milk
- 1/2 cup firmly packed
  brown sugar

Cinnamon Sugar:

- 1/3 cup firmly packed
  brown sugar
- 1 teaspoon cinnamon
- 1/4 teaspoon nutmeg

EQUIPMENT

large saucepan with lid
dry-ingredient
  measuring cups
measuring spoons
liquid measuring cup
wooden spoon
small bowl

Ask an adult to help you prepare this recipe.

1. In saucepan over medium-high heat, combine 1 cup rice, 1/4 teaspoon salt, and 2 cups water. Bring mixture to boil. Reduce heat to low. Cover and cook for 12 to 15 minutes, or until all water is absorbed.

2. Gently stir in 4 cups milk and 1/2 cup brown sugar until well mixed.

3. Turn heat to medium. Stir constantly until mixture just begins to bubble.

4. Reduce heat to low. Cover and cook for 45 to 50 minutes, stirring every 3 to 5 minutes until mixture is creamy and thick.

5. Meanwhile, prepare cinnamon sugar. In bowl, combine 1/3 cup brown sugar, 1 teaspoon cinnamon, and 1/4 teaspoon nutmeg. Set aside.

6. When rice is done, remove from heat. Dish into bowls and sprinkle with cinnamon sugar. Serve immediately.

Makes 6 to 8 servings.

PRESERVING FRUIT

Fruit needed to be preserved quickly before it spoiled. Pioneers dried and canned fruit. They dried sliced apples, peaches, pears, and melons in the sun. Fruits were dried, broken into pieces, and stored in sacks or **crocks**. In winter months pioneers ate the dried fruit as a snack. They also soaked the dry fruit in water to make **pulp** for pies and cakes.

Pioneers canned chunks of fruit in sugar syrup or mashed the fruit to make jams. Women made fruit spreads such as apple, pumpkin, and plum butters. Chokecherries could be made into a tasty jelly or syrup that was a favorite with pioneer families. Some prairie pioneers made **marmalade** from cantaloupes or muskmelons.

Many women preserved whole or sliced fruit in sugar syrup. They packed peaches, apples, and cherries covered in sugar syrup in tightly sealed jars. The jars of jams, jellies, and butters kept throughout the winter until the next year's harvest.

crock—a thick earthenware pot or jar
pulp—the soft, juicy, or fleshy part of fruits and vegetables
marmalade—a kind of jam made from citrus fruits or melons

SPICED APPLE BUTTER

INGREDIENTS

3 pounds (about 6) medium apples
3 cups firmly packed brown sugar
1-1/2 teaspoons cinnamon
1/2 teaspoon allspice
1/2 teaspoon nutmeg
1/2 teaspoon cloves
1/8 teaspoon salt

EQUIPMENT

cutting board
sharp knife
Dutch oven or large saucepan
dry-ingredient measuring cups
wooden spoon
food processor or blender
4 (8-ounce) jars or 2 pint jars

Ask an adult to help you prepare this recipe.

1. Chop apples. Remove cores. Do not peel.

2. In Dutch oven or saucepan, combine all ingredients. Cook over medium-high heat 20 minutes or until hot and bubbly.

3. Reduce heat to medium-low. Cook uncovered about 1-1/2 hours, stirring frequently, until apples are very tender and liquid has thickened.

4. Remove from heat. Cool 10 minutes. Place small batches of apples with liquid in food processor or blender. Blend until mixture is smooth and thick.

5. Pour into jars with tight-fitting lids.

6. Serve when desired with bread or toast.

7. Apple butter will remain fresh for up to 1 month in refrigerator or up to 6 months in freezer.

Makes 4 cups apple butter.

CHAPTER 7

SMOKEHOUSES, ROOT CELLARS, AND ICEHOUSES

Pioneers kept meat in smokehouses. They stacked barrels of salt pork and beef jerky in the smokehouse. Shelves inside held crocks of sausage patties and links of ring sausage. Pioneers hung hams, beefsteaks, and roasts in the smokehouse.

The root cellar was a hole dug out of the ground or into the side of a hill. The size of root cellars varied. The root cellar could be a shallow hole or the size of a small room. This storage spot contained jars of canned fruits and vegetables, sacks of flour, cornmeal, wheat, dried vegetables, and bundles of dried herb and spice plants. Pioneers also stored potatoes, sweet potatoes, and **rutabagas** in the root cellar.

During the winter many types of food were stored in an **icehouse**. They cut slabs of ice from nearby ponds or rivers. Pioneers then stacked the slabs between layers of straw in the icehouse. Milk, eggs, and meat were placed next to the blocks of ice to keep them from spoiling.

rutabaga—a turnip with a large yellowish root that is eaten as a vegetable
icehouse—a small building where pioneers stored chunks of ice and food

FRIED POTATOES

INGREDIENTS

4 to 5 medium potatoes
water
1 small onion
3 tablespoons vegetable oil
1/2 teaspoon salt
1/4 teaspoon pepper

EQUIPMENT

Dutch oven or large saucepan
liquid measuring cup
cutting board
sharp knife
large skillet or electric skillet
measuring spoons
spatula

Ask an adult to help you prepare this recipe.

1. Place potatoes in Dutch oven or saucepan. Cover with water. Boil 20 minutes. Let cool.

2. Peel potatoes. Cut potatoes into 1/4-inch (0.6-cm) slices.

3. Peel skin from onion. Cut onion into 1/4-inch (0.6-cm) slices.

4. In skillet, heat 3 tablespoons oil over medium-high heat. Add onion slices and cook 4 to 5 minutes or until onions are tender. Remove pan from heat.

5. Add sliced potatoes, 1/2 teaspoon salt, and 1/4 teaspoon pepper with onions.

6. Lower heat to medium. Cook uncovered 4 minutes. Flip potatoes and let brown. Cook 4 to 6 minutes or until all potatoes have crisp edges and are tender. If you are able to easily stick a fork through a potato, the potato is tender.

Makes 6 servings.

CHAPTER 8

PARTIES AND SOCIALS

Pioneers took a break from work to celebrate special occasions. Many participated in fairs and attended picnics on the Fourth of July. Communities organized concerts and harvesting parties. The main holiday most pioneers celebrated was Christmas.

Preparations began two to three weeks before Christmas Eve. The community gathered at the schoolhouse to choose a Christmas tree. Children strung popcorn and made paper chains for decorations.

On Christmas Day pioneers served a large dinner of turkey, goose, and ham. They baked fresh bread, rolls, and biscuits. They had pies, cakes, and pastries for dessert.

As communities grew, basket socials became popular. Events were held to raise money for the schoolhouse or the church. Women packed baskets of fried chicken, rolls, cakes, and coffee. An **auctioneer** sold the baskets to the person who bid the most money. That pioneer would then share the basket lunch with the woman who made it.

auctioneer—a person who runs a sale where goods are sold to the person who bids the most money for them

MOLASSES SNOW CONES

INGREDIENTS

1/2 cup dark molasses
1/3 cup firmly packed
    light brown sugar
About 4-1/2 cups crushed ice*
6 (6-ounce) paper cups

EQUIPMENT

liquid measuring cup
small saucepan
dry-ingredient
    measuring cups

wooden spoon
measuring spoons
blender
bowl

Ask an adult to help you prepare this recipe.

1. In saucepan, combine 1/2 cup molasses
   and 1/3 cup brown sugar.

2. Heat over medium-high heat, stirring
   frequently, about 2 minutes or until mixture
   is smooth and thickened. Cool slightly.

3. Spoon about 3/4 cup crushed ice
   into each paper cup. Drizzle 2 tablespoons
   molasses syrup over each snow cone.

*To make crushed ice:

1. Place 8 ice cubes in blender. Mix at low speed.
   Put crushed ice in bowl.

2. Repeat 3 times; use a total of 36 ice cubes.
   Makes 4-1/2 cups crushed ice.

Tips:

For clean-up, soak pan in hot water to soften syrup.

GLOSSARY

auctioneer (awk-shuh-NEER)—a person who runs a sale where goods are sold to the person who bids the most money for them

buttermilk (BUHT-ur-milk)—the sour liquid left over after butter has been churned from cream

chokecherry (CHOHK-CHER-ee)—a wild cherry with a bitter fruit that is nearly black when ripe

crock (KRAHK)—a thick earthenware pot or jar

Dutch oven (DUHCH-UHV-uhn)—a large covered pot

general store (JEN-ur-uhl STOR)—a store found in a small town, which sells many different things including groceries

harvest (HAR-vist)—to collect or gather up crops

icehouse (EYESS-hous)—a small building where pioneers stored chunks of ice and food

lard (LARD)—a solid white grease made from the melted-down fat of pigs and hogs. Lard is used in cooking

marmalade (MAR-muh-lade)—a kind of jam made from citrus fruits or melons

pulp (PUHLP)—the soft, juicy, or fleshy part of fruits and vegetables

root cellar (ROOT SEL-ur)—a hole dug out of the ground or into the side of a hill. Used to store jars of canned food and bundles of dried herbs and plants

rutabaga (roo-tuh-BEY-guh)—a turnip with a large yellowish root that is eaten as a vegetable

soddy (SOD-ee)—pioneer homes made from stacking strips and blocks of sod

sorghum (SOR-guhm)—a tropical grass that is cultivated for grain, forage, or syrup

territory (TER-uh-tor-ee)—any large area of land; a region

turmeric (TOO-mer-ik)—an Indian herb related to ginger and having a large yellow underground plant stem

water reservoir (WAW-tur REZ-ur-vwar)—a holding area for water or steam

30

READ MORE

Gunderson, Jessica. *Your Life as a Pioneer on the Oregon Trail.* The Way It Was. North Mankato, Minn.: Capstone Press, 2012.

McCarthy, Pat. *Daniel Boone: American Pioneer and Frontiersman.* Legendary American Biographies. Berkeley Heights, N.J.: Enslow Publishers, 2015.

Rajczak, Kristen. *Life as a Pioneer.* What You Didn't Know About History. New York: Gareth Stevens Pub., 2013.

INTERNET SITES

FactHound offers a safe, fun way to find Internet sites related to this book. All of the sites on FactHound have been researched by our staff.

Here's all you do:

Visit *www.facthound.com*

Type in this code: 9781515723554

Check out projects, games and lots more at
www.capstonekids.com

INDEX